To.... my silly Little Pumpkin that is growing up way too fast!!!

. . . .

From.... Luv,
Mike & Carolyn

. . . .

Color Me!
GRAND JOKES FOR GRAND KIDS!

Grandma, can you put my shoes on?

No, I don't think they'll fit me!

How did the human cannonball lose his job?

He got fired!

Why does a baker bake bread?

Because he kneads the dough!

Why did the bird go to hospital?

To get a tweetment!

I'll call you later.

Don't call me later, call me *Grandpa!*

Why do pens get sent to prison?

To do long sentences!

What did the girl say to her grandfather when he fell in the river?

Paddle, pop!

Which type of dog has no tail?

A hotdog!

Hear the joke about the wall?

I can't get over it....

What school subject are snakes best at?

Hiss-tory!

Why shouldn't you take a cow to the zoo?

Because they'd rather go to the moovies!

What did the mama cow say to the baby cow?

It's *pasture* bedtime!

Why didn't the skeleton go to the party?

He had *no-body* to go with!

What do snowmen call their kids?

Chill-dren!

What does the carpet salesman give to his wife for Valentine's Day?

Rugs and kisses!

What do you call a crazy golfer?

A crack putt!

What lies in a pram and wobbles?

A jelly baby!

What do they sing at a snowman's birthday party?

Freeze a jolly good fellow!

What's the most popular gardening magazine in the world?

Weeder's Digest!

What is green and sits in the corner?

A naughty frog!

How do monkeys make toast?

They stick some bread under the *gorilla!*

What lies at the bottom of the sea and shivers?

A nervous wreck!

What kind of room has no windows or doors?

A mushroom!

What do you call cattle with a sense of humor?

Laughing stock!

What's the best thing about being 103 years old?

No peer pressure!

How do you hire a horse?

Stand it on four bricks!

Why did the scientist install a knocker on his door?

He wanted to win the no-bell prize!

What do you get if you cross a snowman
with a shark?

Frostbite!

What do you get if you cross a skeleton
with a detective?

Sherlock Bones!

What do you get if you cross a stereo
with a refrigerator?

Cool music!

Who invented fractions?

Henry the 1/8th!

What do elves learn at school?

The elf-abet!

Who delivers presents to dogs?

Santa Paws!

Who says, "oh, oh, oh"?

Santa walking backwards!

What do you get if you cross a bell with a skunk?

Jingle Smells!

Why do grasshoppers not go to football matches?

They prefer cricket matches!

Without geometry life is **pointless!**

What do you call a deer with no eyes?

No idea!

What do you get if you cross a chicken with a cement mixer?

A brick-layer!

Why do birds fly south in winter?

Because it's too far to walk!

What are the small rivers that run into the Nile?

The juve-niles!

How did the Vikings send secret messages?

By Norse code!

What do ghosts eat?

Spookghetti!

What do hedgehogs eat?

Prickled onions!

What do you call two robbers?

A pair of knickers!

What cereals do cats like?

Mice Krispies!

Why does a spider bring toilet paper to a party?

Because he is a party pooper!

What do you call an elephant that never washes?

A smellyphant!

Why are skeletons so calm?

Because nothing gets under their skin!

Why do scuba divers fall backwards
into the water?

If they fell forwards they'd still be in the boat!

What do you call a deer with no eyes *and* no legs?

Still no idea!

What do vampires sing on New Year's Eve?

Auld *Fang* Syne!

What's the fastest thing in water?

A motor pike!

What do you get if you cross a cowboy with an octopus?

Billy the Squid!

Why is Europe like a frying pan?

Because it has *Greece* at the bottom!

What's Tarzan's favorite song?

Jungle Bells!

How does a snowman travel around?

By riding an icicle!

Where do snow-women like to dance?

At snowballs!

What do snowmen wear on their heads?

Ice caps!

Why was the snowman looking through the carrots?

He was picking his nose!

Why does it take pirates so long to learn the alphabet?

Because they can spend years at c!

What is black and white and noisy?

A zebra with a drum kit!

Why did the man get the sack from the orange juice factory?

Because he couldn't concentrate!

How do bubbles communicate?

By mobile foam!

Why did the mechanic sleep under the car?

He wanted to get up *oily* in the morning!

Why did the bull wear a bell?

Because his horn didn't work!

How do you make a bandstand?

Hide all the chairs!

What do you get when you cross a sheep with a kangaroo?

A woolly jumper!

What happens when you throw a stone into
the red sea?
It gets wet.

What's white and dangerous?
A fridge falling out of the sky!

What do you call a man with no nose and no body?
Nobody nose!

I cut my finger chopping cheese, but I think
that I may have ***grater*** problems!

A man walks into a bar ....**ouch!**

Which animal talks the most?

A yak!

What's faster, hot or cold?

Hot, because you can catch a cold!

What do you call a man with a pole in his leg?

Rod-ney!

What do you call a snowman in the summer time?

A puddle!

What is the best present you can receive?

A broken drum. You can't beat it!

What did Adam say the day before Christmas?

It's Christmas, Eve!

What table at school doesn't have legs?

The multiplication table!

What's brown and sticky?

A stick!

What's black and white and eats like a horse?

A zebra!

What do you call a dog with no legs?

Nothing, it won't come to you anyway!

What type of fish is the most famous?

A starfish!

How many golfers does it take to change a lightbulb?

Fore!

"Hey, did you get a haircut?"

"No, I got them *all* cut."

What do you call a boomerang that does not come back?

A stick!

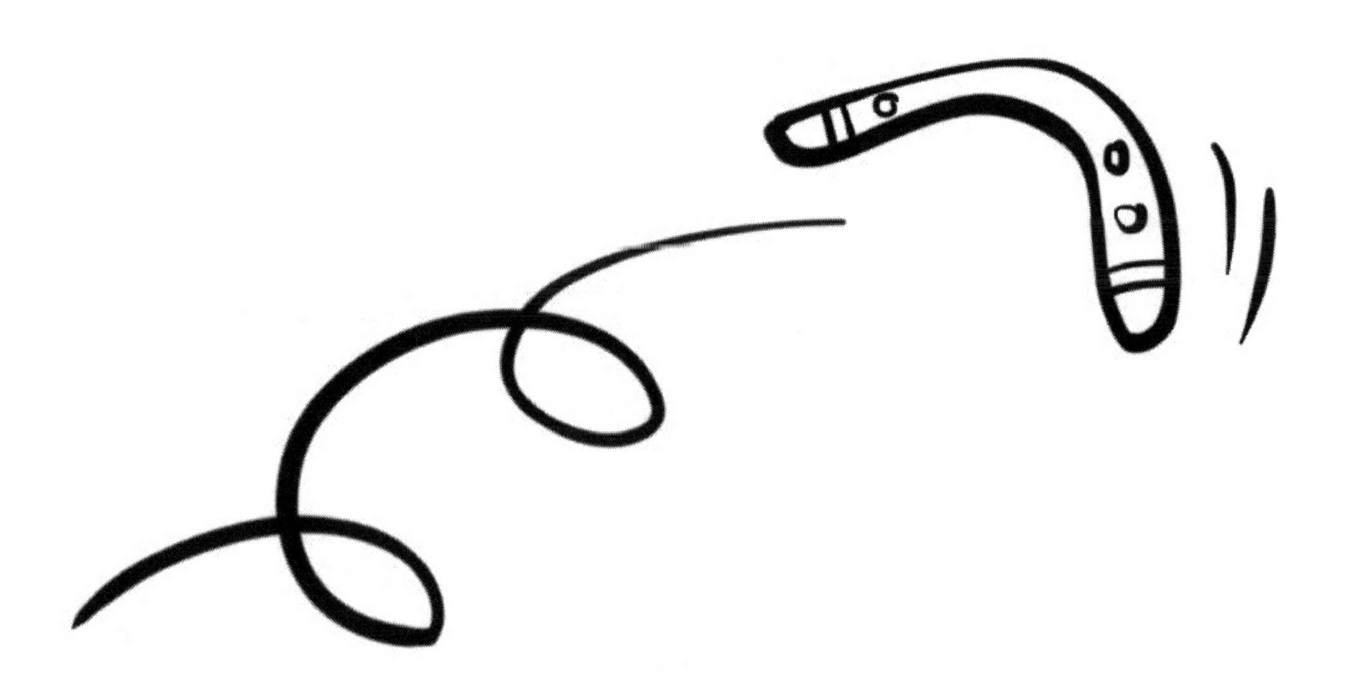

What's red and white?

Pink!

What do you call a man with a shovel?

Doug!

What do you call a man *without* a shovel?

Douglas!

What do you call a man in a pile of leaves?

Russell!

What do you call a lady with one leg?

Ilene!

What do you call a man lying under a car?

Jack!

What do you call a man with no arms and no legs lying in front of your door?

Matt!

Why was the kangaroo mad at her children?

Because they ate biscuits in bed!

What did one flea say to another?

Shall we walk or take a dog?

Why did the tomato blush?

Because he saw the salad dressing!

What does Dracula take when he's sick?

Coffin syrup!

What did Grandma spider say to baby spider?

You spend too much time on the web!

What do you call a group of killer whales
playing instruments?

An orca-stra!

How do hedgehogs kiss?

Very carefully!

What sort of animal needs oil?

Mice, because they squeak!

How long does it take a candle to burn?

About a wick!

Do you know the joke about the butter?

I'm not going to tell you because you'll spread it around!

Why did the tightrope walker go to his bank?

To check his balance!

Why do golfers wear 2 pairs of pants?

In case they get a hole in one!

How do you start a teddy bear race?

Teddy, Set, Go!

What do you call a line of men waiting for a haircut?

A barber-queue!

What sort of TV program do ducks watch?

Duckumentaries!

What did the ocean say to the shore?

Nothing, it just waved!

Why do crabs never give to charity?

Because they're shellfish!

What kind of magic do cows believe in?

MOODOO!

What time is it?

I don't know. It keeps changing!

What is blue and smells like red paint?

Blue paint!

What do clouds wear?

Thunderwear!

What invention lets you see through walls?

Windows!

What was the tortoise doing on the freeway?

About 1 mile per hour!

What did the judge say when a skunk was found by the bailiff?

Odor in the court!

How did the man drown in his bowl of muesli?

A strong currant pulled him in!

What do you call a fish with no eyes?

A fsh!

Why was the turkey in the pop group?

Because he was the only one with drumsticks!

I'm reading a book on the history of glue –

I can't put it down!

What did baby corn say to mama corn?

Where's popcorn?

What's the difference between an African elephant

and an Indian elephant?

About 5000 miles!

What do you call a bear without ears?

B

What do hippopotamuses have that

no other animals have?

Baby hippopotamuses!

Why do giraffes have long necks?

Because their feet smell!

What did the fish say when it swam into a wall?

Dam!

What's round and bad tempered?

A vicious circle!

On which side do chickens have the most feathers?

The outside!

What did the policeman say to the stomach?

You're under a vest!

Why is it so difficult to train dogs to dance?

They have two left feet!

What wobbles and flies?

A jelly-copter!

What goes ha, ha, ha clonk?

A man laughing his head off!

What do you get when you cross a cat
with a lemon?

A sour puss!

What athlete is warmest in winter?

A long jumper!

Did you hear about the kidnapping at school?

It's fine, he woke up!

Why'd the belt get arrested?

He held up a pair of pants!

What's the difference between a guitar and a fish?

You can't tuna fish!

Why would you invite a mushroom to a party?

He's a *fun-guy* to be with!

What has four legs but can't walk?

A table!

Why did the hedgehog cross the road?

To see his *flat*-mate!

What goes up and never comes down?

Your age!

What kind of paper likes music?

Rapping paper!

What do you call a woman who stands between two goal posts?

Annette!

Did you hear about the man who bought a paper shop?

It blew away!

How do you make a tissue dance?

Put a boogie in it!

What did the grape say when the elephant stepped on it?

Nothing. It just let out a little wine!

What do you call a belt with a watch on it?

A *waist* of time!

An invisible man marries an invisible woman.

The kids were not much to look at either!

This graveyard looks overcrowded. People must be *dying* to get in there!

Why move to Switzerland?

Well, the flag is a big plus!

What time is it when you need to see a dentist?

Tooth-hurty!

How do you stop a skunk smelling?

Hold its nose!

Which country has the largest appetite?

Hungary!

What do spacemen play in their spare time?

Astronauts and crosses!

How do you make an octopus laugh?

Ten tickles!

What do you call a zebra with no stripes?

A horse!

What do you get when you cross an elephant and a potato?

Mashed potatoes!

Why did the turkey cross the road?

Because he wasn't chicken!

What's orange and sounds like a parrot?

A carrot!

What do you call a blind dinosaur?

A do-you-think-he-saw-us!

'Should I call a *toe* truck?' Granddad asks every time I stub my toe!

What do you call a penguin in the Sahara desert?

Lost!

What do you call a sleeping bull?

A bull-dozer!

What do you call a train filled with toffee?

A *chew chew* train!

Where do astronauts leave their cars?

At parking meteors!

Why are pines trees bad at sewing?

Because they are always dropping their needles!

Where do sheep get their hair cut?

At the *baa baa* shop!

Why can't a car play football?

Because they only have one boot!

Where do ghosts go swimming?

In the Dead Sea!

What does a frog do if his car breaks down?

He gets it toad away!

What do you call a three-legged donkey?

A wonky donkey!

How do hens encourage their baseball teams?

They egg them on!

What tea do hockey players drink?

Penaltea!

Nostalgia isn't what it used to be!

Why can't a leopard hide?

Because they are always spotted!

How do you count cows?

With a *cow*-culator!

How do you talk to fish?

Drop them a line!

Why is the cemetery such a noisy place?

Because of all the *coffin!*

What do you get if you cross a Christmas tree with an apple?

A pine-apple!

How do you organize a space party?

You planet!

Why did the scarecrow win an award?

Because he was outstanding in his field!

Did you hear about the new restaurant
on the Moon?
**The food was great, but there was just
no atmosphere!**

I was thinking about moving to Moscow...
But there's no point in *Russian* into things!

What do you get when you cross a naughty sheep
and a grumpy cow?
An animal that's in a baaaaaaaad mooooooood!

What do cows get when they're sick?
Hay fever!

How does a cow get to the moon?
It flies through udder space!

What do you call a monkey with a banana in each ear?

Anything you want, it can't hear you!

What did the buffalo say when his son left?

Bison!

How did the octopus beat a shark in a fight?

He was well armed!

I'm afraid for the calendar. . .

Its days are numbered!

A sandwich walks into a bar.

Bartender says, **"Sorry, we don't serve food here!"**

Why did the pony need a glass of water?

He was a little *hoarse!*

You hear about the new broom?

It's sweeping the nation!

Why didn't the skeleton cross the road?

It didn't have the guts!

Velcro?

What a rip-off!

This documentary about beavers is the best ***dam*** thing I've ever watched!

What do you call a man with a rubber toe?

Roberto!

What do you call a fat psychic?

A four-chin teller!

I am terrified of elevators.

I'm going to start ***taking steps*** to avoid them!

What do you call a bear with no teeth?

A gummy bear!

Why do you smear peanut butter on the road?

To go with the traffic jam!

What do you call the cat who was caught by the police?

The purrpetrator!

Why don't cats like online shopping?

They prefer cat-alogs!

What did the cat say when he lost his toys?

You got to be kitten me!

What's a cat's favorite color?

Purrrrrple!

What happened to the lion who ate the comedian?

He felt funny!

What is a French cat's favorite pudding?

Chocolate mousse!

What did the alien say to the cat?

Take me to your litter!

How does a dog stop a film?

By hitting the *paws* button!

What do you call a cow you can't see?

Ca-moo-flaged!

Where do cows go for lunch?

The calf-eteria!

How many apples grow on a tree?

All of them!

Why did the old man fall in the well?

Because he couldn't see that well!

What's a cat's favorite TV show?

The evening mews!

What did the cat say when he lost all his money?

I'm paw!

What looks like half a cat?

The other half!

Want to hear a joke about paper?

Never mind, it's *tear-able*!

Why did the coffee file a police report?

It got mugged!

Want to hear a joke about construction?

I'm still working on it!

The **shovel** was a *ground-breaking* invention!

Granddad, can you put the cat out?

I didn't know it was on fire!

Cashier: 'Would you like the milk in a bag?'

Me: **'No, just leave it in the carton!'**

5/4 of people admit that they're **bad** with fractions!

Two goldfish are in a tank. One says to the other,

"do you know how to drive this thing!?"

I used to work in a shoe recycling shop.

It was *soul* destroying!

What do you get from a pampered cow?

Spoiled milk!

What do lawyers wear to court?

Lawsuits!

How does a bear catch a fish without a fishing pole?

With its *bear* hands!

I would avoid the sushi if I was you.

It's a little fishy!

The *rotation* of Earth really makes my **day**!

I thought about going on an all cashew diet.

But that's just nuts!

Why do you never see elephants hiding in trees?

Because they're so good at it!

What is the highest form of flattery?

A plateau!

A Spanish magician says that he'll disappear on the count of three.

"Uno... dos..." **POOF!**

He disappeared without a ***tres!***

I don't have to play soccer.

I'm just doing it for kicks!

Me: 'Hey, I was thinking...'

My Grandma: **'I thought I smelled something burning!'**

How does a penguin build its house?

Igloos it together!

How can you tell if an ant is a boy or a girl?

They're all girls, otherwise they'd be uncles!

I walked past a graveyard with my Granddad and he said, 'Do you know why I can't be buried there?'

I asked, 'Why not?'

And Granddad replies, **'Because I'm not dead yet!'**

Why did the dog not want to play football?

It was a boxer!

I had a job at a calendar factory but I got the sack because I took a couple of ***days off!***

Wow, you're a ***fart smella***...I mean ***smart fella!***

I had a dream that I was a muffler last night. I woke up ***exhausted!***

What is Beethoven's favorite fruit?

A ba-na-na-na!

What did the right eye say to the left eye?

Between you and me, something smells!

What did the pirate say on his 80th birthday?

Aye 'maighty!

What do you call a clever duck?

A wise quack!

Why do pandas like old movies?

Because they're in black and white!

4, 6, 8, and 9 have all been kidnapped,

2, 3, 5, 7, and 11 are the **prime suspects!**

What did one snowman say to the other one?

Do you smell carrots?

If your nose *runs* and your feet *smell*, you are built

upside down!

What gets wetter the more it dries?

A towel!

What's a teacher's favorite nation?

Expla-nation!

What do you call a frozen dog?

A pup-sicle!

What do you call a cold dog?

A *chili* dog!

Where did the dog park his car?

In the *barking* lot!

What do you call a monkey with a bomb?

A *ba-boom!*

What kind of key opens a banana?

A *mon-key!*

Why did the monkey like the banana?

Because it had *appeal!*

What did the banana do when he saw the monkey?

The banana split!

Where do the chimps get their gossip?

On the *ape* vine!

What do you call a baby monkey?

A chimp off the old block!

What's the king of all school supplies?

The ruler!

How do baseball players stay cool?

They sit next to their fans!

How did the basketball get wet?

The players dribbled all over it!

What kind of shoes does a thief wear?

Sneakers!

At what time does a duck wake up?

At the quack of dawn!

What did Detective Duck say to his partner?

Let's quack this case!

What do you call a duck that steals?

A robber ducky!

What did the duck say when the waitress came?

Put it on my bill!

Where did the duck go when he was sick?

To the ducktor!

How do ducks talk?

They don't, you quack!

What do you call a sheep with no legs?

A cloud!

What do you call a wet bear?

A drizzly bear!

Why don't bears like fast food?

Because they can't catch it!

What is a pirate's favorite store?

The second-hand store!

What has 8 eyes, 8 arms, & 8 legs?

Four rookie pirates!

How does a pirate clean his house?

He has a yaaaaarrrrrd sale!

What's a pirate's favorite kind of fish?

A gold-fish!

What's a chalkboard's favorite drink?

Hot chalk-olate!

Why is a cyclops such an effective teacher?

He only has one pupil!

Why did the student throw his watch out the window?

He wanted to see time fly!

Why shouldn't you do math in the jungle?

Because if you add 4+4 you get *ate!*

What happened to the plant in math class?

It grew square roots!

What do a hockey player and a magician have in common?

They both do hat tricks!

What can you serve but never eat?

A volleyball!

Why did the chicken get sent off?

For fowl play!

What should a soccer team do if the field is flooded?

Bring on their subs!

Which insect did not play well as quarterback?

The fumble-bee!

What's a tennis player's favorite city?

Volleywood!

Why can't you hear a pterodactyl using the bathroom?

Because the P is silent!

Why did the students take ladders to school?

Because they were going to high school!

What's a runner's favorite subject at school?

Jog-raphy!

What do you call a cow who plays a musical instrument?

A moo-sician!

What did one Japanese man say to the other?

I don't know, I can't speak Japanese!

What do you call a fake noodle?

An impasta!

Why did the picture go to jail?

It was framed!

What do you call a pile of kittens?

A meowntain!

Did you hear about the shampoo shortage
in Jamaica?
It's dread-full!

Did you hear about the hungry clock?
It went back four seconds!

Me, 'Can I watch the TV?'
Granddad, 'Yes, but don't turn it on!'

What did the mountain climber name his son?
Cliff!

I went to buy some *camouflage* trousers the other day, but I couldn't **find** any!

I went to a seafood disco last week... **and pulled a mussel!**

Did you hear about the man who stole a calendar?

He got 12 months!

Which big cat was disqualified from the race?

The cheetah!

'Doctor, I've broken my arm in several places!'

'Well, don't go to those places.'

Slept like a log last night ... **woke up in the fireplace!**

A man woke up in a hospital after a serious accident.

He shouted, 'Doctor, I can't feel my legs!"

The doctor replied, 'I know you can't. **I've cut off your arms!'**

I knew I shouldn't have eaten that seafood.

Because now I'm feeling a little... **Eel!**

What did the 0 say to the 8?

Nice belt!

'Ahh, this takes me back,' Grandma says every time she reverses the car!

'Be careful standing near those trees.'

'Why?'

'They just look kind of shady to me!'

Where is the dead center of town?

The cemetery!

Why couldn't the bike stand on its own?

Because it was *two tired*!

I don't trust stairs.

They're always up to something!

If a child refuses to take a nap, is he resisting ***a rest***?

Want to hear my pizza joke?

Never mind, it's too cheesy!

What does a house wear?

A-ddress!

What is blue and doesn't weigh very much?

Light blue!

They're finally making a film about clocks...

It's about time!

I couldn't figure out why the baseball kept getting larger. **Then it hit me.**

What did the janitor say when he jumped out of the closet?

Supplies!

I used to be afraid of hurdles...

Then I got over them!

My friend asked me to help him round up his 37 sheep.

I said 40!

I have an addiction to cheddar cheese...

But it's only mild!

Did you hear about the magic tractor?

It was driving down the road and turned into a field!

I'm only familiar with 25 letters in the English language...

I don't know why!

Nothing rhymes with 'orange'.

No, it doesn't!

My friend recently got crushed by a pile of books...

But he has only got his shelf to blame!

Sometimes I tuck my knees into my chest and lean forward...

That's just how I roll!

What does a zombie vegetarian eat?

GRAAAAAINS!!!!

I don't trust atoms...

They make up everything!

What vitamin helps your vision?

Vitamin C.

When do astronauts eat?

At launch time!

What animal can jump higher than a house?

Most animals. A house can't jump!

What do you call a broken pencil?

Pointless!

What do sea monsters eat?

Fish and ships!

74427972R00046

Made in the USA
Lexington, KY
14 December 2017